teetering in the unknown

*

travel-induced lessons, knowledge, and allegories

Katherine Scott

United States

© 2020 Katherine Scott

All rights reserved.

No part of this book, in printed form or in digital form,
may be reproduced
in any way without written permission
from the publisher.

Published in the United States.

www.teeteringintheunknownbook.com

First Edition
Print

The journey changes you; it should change you.
It leaves marks on your memory, on your consciousness,
on your heart, and on your body.
You take something with you.
Hopefully, you leave something good behind.

Anthony Bourdain

CONTENTS

introduction

I. Travel as Food | 11

II. Travel as Art | 19

III. Travel as Self Care | 31

IV. Travel as Fear | 43

V. Travel as Immortality | 53

VI. Travel as Philosophy | 65

VII. Travel as Home | 81

Acknowledgments

Credits

About the Author

Ithaka

As you set out for Ithaka
hope your road is a long one,
full of adventure, full of discovery.
Laistrygonians, Cyclops,
angry Poseidon—don't be afraid of them:
you'll never find things like that on your way
as long as you keep your thoughts raised high,
as long as a rare excitement
stirs your spirit and your body.
Laistrygonians, Cyclops,
wild Poseidon—you won't encounter them
unless you bring them along inside your soul,
unless your soul sets them up in front of you.

Hope your road is a long one.
May there be many summer mornings when,
with what pleasure, what joy,
you enter harbors you're seeing for the first time;
may you stop at Phoenician trading stations
to buy fine things,
mother of pearl and coral, amber and ebony,
sensual perfume of every kind—
as many sensual perfumes as you can;
and may you visit many Egyptian cities
to learn and go on learning from their scholars.

Keep Ithaka always in your mind.
Arriving there is what you're destined for.
But don't hurry the journey at all.
Better if it lasts for years,
so you're old by the time you reach the island,
wealthy with all you've gained on the way,
not expecting Ithaka to make you rich.

Ithaka gave you the marvelous journey.
Without her you wouldn't have set out.
She has nothing left to give you now.

And if you find her poor, Ithaka won't have fooled you.
Wise as you will have become, so full of experience,
you'll have understood by then what these Ithakas mean.

By C.P. Cavafy
Translated by Edmund Kelley

INTRODUCTION

This is not a travel memoir. This is not a how-to book, or a guide to fulfilling a bucket list. This is not a book of essays, a novel, or a list of must-see places around the globe. You will find very little advice on these pages. I do not provide an outline on how to travel solo, and I do not offer compendiums of the cheapest international airlines and hotels. There is no mention of the most Instagram-worthy streets in Paris, and whether you should bring a neck pillow on a flight will not be covered.

If you want any of that information, simply Google the word "travel." You might find blog articles called *The Portugal Must-See Guide, The Perfect Iceland Itinerary for 3 Days,* or *The Top 10 Pho Restaurants of Southeast Asia.* These articles contain immense information. Carefully timed city walks that cover all the major landmarks, the best days to buy flights, gastronomic city tours that include Michelin star restaurants, street food, and everything in between. No small amount of research went into the creation of these types of travel articles.

The information is detailed and tedious; but, is it worth anything to you? It isn't to me.

This book contains lessons, themes, allegories, mistakes, and knowledge that I've come across while traveling. I've made a concerted effort not to simply retell my favorite stories or to tell you how to travel. As it is, my trips have been my own experiences, not yours. And I'm not here to brag or preach.

Rather, I've created something abstract as a means of sharing my personal experiences. I don't want to label my own ways as the gold standard of travel. Sometimes, in fact, my way of traveling is a good example of what *not* to do.

Whether or not you agree with my testimony, I hope to persuade you to travel more often, with more depth, and with less expectation than before. After all, we are not here to live a perfect life or to go on the perfect adventure, but rather to live fiercely imperfectly while enjoying the ride.

I.
TRAVEL
AS
FOOD

People who love to eat are always the best people.

Julia Child

THE CHARCUTERIE OF TRAVEL

When arranging a charcuterie board, one must make many decisions. There are aesthetics, flavors, textures, and pairings to consider. The types of cheese should differ in hardness, sharpness, and animal of origin to provide a complex spread. The meats offer another set of flavors to both elevate and accompany the cheeses. Chorizo, salami, cured ham, pepperoni, sausage. Each provides a distinct smokiness, pepperiness, or saltiness and gives the cheese a unique companion.

The next layer of the board includes olives, grapes, berries, and nuts. Olives require the eater to slow down in order to remove all the glorious olive meat from the pit. The grapes, berries, and nuts offer sprinklings of sweetness and saltiness here and there.

The final layer is the finishing touches. A small pot of fig preserve and another of honey, a dish of extra virgin olive oil with a dash of salt, crisp baguette cut on the bias, rosemary crackers, whole clementines. These provide the vehicles upon which the cheese and meats enter the mouth, while adorning the board with additional depth. They allow the eater to get creative in their cracker towers by combining various components of the board into one bite. They are not necessary for the board to constitute charcuterie, but they make it exceptionally delightful and rich.

Now let's consider the charcuterie of travel. Aesthetics aside, you must consider where to go on your trip. What location can provide you with the same variety that a spread of cheeses can? Do you prefer a hard city? A soft countryside? A rich coast?

Who will accompany you on this trip? The company can either make your trip unforgettable or rather regrettable. Certain locations lend themselves to certain groups. Will this be a romantic trip? A life-changing mission? A soul-searching solo adventure? Sometimes, like cheese, you're better off alone.

While on your trip, you will experience ups and downs. A lovely day spent strolling the streets of a new city will eventually end. Flights get delayed, trains run late, and baggage gets lost. Par for the course. Patience, resilience, and a good attitude go miles. Literally. So enjoy the sweet moments as they happen, for what is coming will come, and it's not important right now.

Little comforts and luxuries can make a trip extra special. These aren't necessary for the trip to happen, but like *fleur de sel* on a charcuterie board, they are just nice to have. Buying the expensive bottle at dinner. Booking the room with a view of the countryside. Ordering the chocolate soufflé. Do whatever makes you smile, because it's your trip and it should be to your taste.

As you create charcuterie boards throughout your life, you realize it's hard to get it wrong. Sure, triple cream cheese pairs divinely with the local raw honey you found at the farmer's market. And the imported mimolette is a perfect companion to the thyme crisps you baked from scratch. But, sometimes the curated combination of flavors isn't what you want. Sometimes, spontaneously mixing flavors and textures results in a much more flavorful, colorful, and memorable bite.

Planning has its time and place. But once in a while, and maybe much more often than that, it's better to just wing it and see how it comes out.

BERBERECHOS

Walking along the knee-deep *orilla*, Rosa reaches into the clear water and picks out a *berberecho*. She breaks it apart with a shell of another, and eats it raw.

I'm staring in awe.

She reaches down again and picks out another. *¿Quieres probar?*

Rosa shows me how to open the *berberecho* and offers it to me in the shell. It's alive. So am I.

Salty and like home, it's the taste of Muros.

THE MORE I EAT, THE BETTER I THINK

THE CROISSANT'S LAMENT

If you are going to feel guilty about eating something as godly as a fresh croissant, save yourself the pain and just don't eat it. Do not for one moment consider the calories you are ingesting as the rich, flaky, buttery, ambrosia-like dough hits your lips. Instead, here are some things to think about as your mouth salivates and your mind spasms at the mere whiff of the fluffy and decadent croissant:

I. The debate of Deconstructionism in literature and where, exactly, you stand on the matter
II. Why did the Romans water down their wine?
III. If Heaven is up and Hell is down, do we live in Purgatory?
IV. What on earth happened to Louis XVI's keys?
V. Whether you believe in Jesus, the man
VI. Whether you believe in Jesus, the son of God
VII. Why don't bomb and tomb rhyme?
VIII. The list of dead people you wish you could meet
IX. How does karma tie into string theory?
X. Whether you like the theoretical or practical side of drinking more

II.
TRAVEL
AS
ART

The most beautiful things in the world cannot be seen or touched, they are felt with the heart.

Antoine de Saint-Exupéry

CUBISM

There are eight museums dedicated to Pablo Picasso worldwide. Three in France, one in Germany, and four in Spain.

Laying eyes on some of the most well known work in history is an unparalleled experience. Like tasting wine straight from the barrel, there is nothing quite like it.

Seeing Picasso's work in a museum is certainly that experience. However, like any artist's work, looking at the final product is not the truest way to evaluate, empathize, or understand it.

Cubism is abandoning a single viewpoint. It's breaking apart expectations and introducing a misunderstood reality. It's changing the surface to better understand the interior. It's seeming absurd, but really being transparently clear.

Adopting the principles of Cubism into the study of Picasso is necessary. However, it might not occur to the museumgoer hurrying through the Museu Picasso on a whirlwind trip to Barcelona. Just laying eyes on the artwork is not the same as seeing the object like the artist did.

Breaking apart the object and abandoning a single viewpoint can hardly be done by just standing in front of *La Baigneuse* in a crowded gallery. The museumgoer must adopt the defining principles of Cubism in order to gain a more satisfying appreciation for Picasso's works.

Aimlessly walk around Montmartre for an afternoon.

Visit the seashore and skim over a book in French.

Close your eyes and imagine the damage the Spanish Civil War had on the country and its people. Open your eyes and see *Guernica*, but not as Picasso depicted it. See it as an actual event that he portrayed so deeply and intensely, it's nearly romantic.

On your next museum trip, as you gaze at a world renowned artifact, wonder what version of reality lies before you. What was really there, sitting in front of the artist? What was added in or left out? What has been morphed? How was this thing significant? Was it significant at all? But most of all, leave the museum and try to experience the art for yourself.

In your own way, forget about the surface and focus on the interior.

THE LADIES IN WAITING

As I entered the Prado with my two friends, I knew it was a bad idea. Tired and hungry, I was the human manifestation of a monster.

But I needed to see *Las Meninas* with my own eyes. The museum was closing in less than an hour, and I was going to power through. All I needed was one short, but analytical, look, and I would be satisfied.

We rushed through the gauntlet of tourists to reach the room where *Las Meninas* stood. *The Ladies in Waiting*, in English, is a grand portrait of both artistic and existential significance. Legend says that looking at this portrait makes the viewer feel an immense sadness. *Duende.*

I had studied this painting for an entire semester, knew each of its components, its meanings, its essential and enduring questions. I just needed to see it with my own eyes so we could leave and eat.

It was just what I had expected. A little larger, perhaps, but it looked exactly like the photos. A minute or two of viewing it, and I felt comfortable with moving on. Done. Like seeing the Eiffel Tower. Glad I saw it, but not the best thing I will see.

As I turned and walked away, I took a final punch in the gut with exhaustion. I looked around and saw a gorgeous corridor, covered in priceless paintings from centuries past. I saw packs of .

people. I saw my two friends. Everything was spinning.

I had to get out. The exhilaration of seeing *Las Meninas* had exited my body, and I was left with the feeling of absolute lifelessness. Choking on my own throat, I could barely speak. *I need to leave*, I tried to tell my friends. Clearly on the verge of tears, they tried to sit me down on a viewing bench. I told them no. I had to leave and eat something, I was going to pass out. They forced me onto the bench which is where I finally broke.

About 15 hours earlier, I had been in a much better place. Dancing the night away with my friends. A tall, blonde Spanish boy with a smile on his face. A bar called Paniagua.

That all seemed like a dream now, as I sat miserable on that bench. I cried. I cried for a bed. For a meal. For love. Then, like the people in the portraits surrounding me, I sat there motionless. The catharsis was over.

Two hugs and many deep breaths later, my own ladies in waiting got me up and we left in search of dinner.

The legend of *Las Meninas* was real.

And so was the deluxe cheeseburger that shortly followed.

a church sits in the middle

of a Mallorquín patio

the bells don't ring

and the choir doesn't sing

the residents gaze

and the visitors wonder

what a curious little place

to be

THE PORTUGUESE ARMOIRE

I arrive in Lisbon, tired, lonely, and scared. Pedro picks me up at the airport. A cool cat. Wears a fedora in a seemingly Portuguese way. One foot up on the bench with arms crossed, leaning over. Sunglasses. Maybe a toothpick?

We get in his Smart Car and now I'm not scared anymore. I'm petrified. We're going 120 km per hour in this shopping cart of a vehicle and it's clear how I will die.

How fast is 120 km per hour anyway? 200 mph?

My dead ancestors must have performed a miracle on my behalf because one hour later we arrive in Cascais intact. Cascais is the earthly version of the Elysian Fields and is no place for panic, worry, or negativity. Which are exactly what I bring along.

Pedro shows me into the apartment. A fairly large bedroom with a small balcony, and a shared bathroom and living area. He's hospitable and warm. But certain implications are passing through my mind. I've agreed to let a complete stranger pick me up at the airport in his miniature car and drive me to a small beach town in Portugal. I'll be staying in his apartment with him as a roommate. There are no knobs on the doors, just towels pulled through the holes where doorknobs should be. What have I gotten myself into?

He leaves me alone to rest and it's exactly what I need. A five hour delayed overnight flight did something terrible to my face and sanity. I try to fall asleep, but can't. I'm realizing that the next nine weeks abroad, alone, are more than what I can handle. I Facetime my parents to fix it. Crying hysterically and leaving all pride aside, I tell them I've bitten off more than I can chew and want to abandon my plans for the rest of the summer. I'm supposed to travel around Portugal and Spain in a solo endeavor that was my idea, and now I can't do it. I need to bail and come home.

My parents tell me to take a nap, and then get outside and explore, and to stay. I'm blubbering like a child, but I eventually follow their directions. I fall asleep for a few hours. It's barely useful, but a small reset is desperately needed. I get up and message a classmate on Facebook that I knew was in Cascais, too. We decide to meet for dinner around the corner from my apartment, and I pull myself together. Physically, I look horrendous. Face is bloated and red from crying. Eyes are puffy. My body is full of sodium from airplane food. But I throw on some makeup, brush my hair, put on a pink skirt, and walk downstairs.

Hours later, I return to the apartment. Dinner, beach, gelado, a walk along the gorgeous *praias* of Cascais renewed me. I can do this.

In the bedroom, I'm getting ready to go to sleep. Between unpacking my carry on size suitcase and rubbing my bloodshot eyes, I finally look at the room. It's gorgeous.

The bed is the only ordinary piece of furniture. A full or maybe a queen. There's a nightstand made of wood on one side and a desk with a chair on the other. Both are understated at first glance. A deeper look, I can see they are wonderful.

I look towards the window. It's dark out, but I pull open the blinds. Being on the third floor, I look to the gelado shop below. And across the street to the large white Portuguese homes with copper colored balconies and palm trees all over.

I turn back inside and finally see it. The armoire. It's a Greek Goddess standing right there in this apartment bedroom. Immortal. Tall and glorious, it's full of Pedro's sweaters and secrets. I keep it. Not for myself or for my own clothes. But as a memory.

The memory of this armoire went with me for the rest of that summer. I relapsed multiple times over the weeks regarding my confidence and willingness to complete the trip. Many more calls were made home, and many more hysterical crying sessions ensued. But the memory of this armoire for some reason calmed me.

Constant, sturdy, mysterious, full, there.

III.
TRAVEL
AS
SELF CARE

If you think adventure is dangerous, try routine. It's lethal.

Paulo Coelho

MOMENTS OF RESPITE

The first hint of sunrise over the plane's wingtip as you near your destination.

Once checked into your lodging and realizing a new city awaits.

Your first bite of French escargots, *en plein air*.

Almost like...

    I.   The first sip of coffee in the morning
   II.   A freshly made white, fluffy bed
  III.   Basking in the sun of a new summer
  IV.   A bubble bath paired with a glass of bubbly
   V.   Having someone else make you breakfast

FLEEING THE COUNTRY

Rarely anymore do you hear of someone fleeing the country. With social media ubiquitous, running away (most likely in the dead of the night) is absurd.

But hypothetically speaking, could you leave behind all you've ever known, your family, friends, belongings, and customs, and start a new life in a foreign land? Most of us do not even have this option, as our lives demand our presence and we lack the sheer courage of this notion.

Fleeing the country is a seductive idea. Although we might not be able to start a new life in an exotic place, we do have the option of taking a trip to a place representative of an escape. Just a short trip to this place would mean leaving behind our responsibilities, jobs, and routine. Being in this place would be a worry-free respite from the daily tedium.

Sometimes a reset in the form of a trip abroad is just the change we need to return to our lives refreshed and, hopefully, better adjusted to our world.

RULES OF TRAVEL

The first rule of travel is don't be a jerk.

There are no further rules.

FIKA

fika : Swedish
(n.): a daily social custom to enjoy a coffee break

hygge : Danish & Norwegian
(n.): the concept of a cozy lifestyle where one enjoys and savors little pleasures and a warm atmosphere

il dolce far niente : Italian
(n.): the sweetness in doing nothing

lagom : Swedish
(adv.): just the right amount

piano piano : Italian
(adv.): little by little

siesta : Spanish
(n.): the time of day when society closes shops and businesses to enjoy lunch at home and to rest

working lunch: English
(n.): a custom in the United States where workers will continue to do their job during lunch time, often resulting in no eating at all

APEROL SPRITZ

The only guideline of Aperol Spritz imbibing is knowing that you do, in fact, have a limit. It's important to know your personal limit before traveling to a foreign land unsupervised.

However, be forewarned. A positive correlation tends to develop between the number of spritzes consumed and how many more a person wants.

So whether you choose to spritz in an outdoor cafe in a busy city or on the shores of a Swedish archipelago, keep in mind that exceeding your limit can make or break the glorious day you've been handed.

So yes, you should definitely have one more.

# IV.
TRAVEL
AS
FEAR

Do one thing everyday that scares you.

Eleanor Roosevelt

SET SAIL

Take pride in finding your own way.

Be messy. Be brave.

The decision is personal.

Have a plan, then throw it away.

No one else has to understand it.

It might not be what you wanted, expected, or feared.

Be independent.

Feel the pain, then do it anyway.

Roll with it. Let it go.

Be prepared to give up your pride.

Never give up your confidence.

Listen.

Look.

Go back.

MOMENTS OF PANIC

Running through the airport, last call has been made.

Your passport is missing.

Your luggage is lost.

Almost like...
- I. Peeking behind the shower curtain to check for murderers
- II. Getting separated from your mom at the grocery store
- III. Watching too many episodes of *Vikings* right before bed
- IV. Realizing your greatest fear in the form of an incredibly realistic nightmare
- V. Being forced onto a roller coaster that you know you'll hate, and then hating it even more than predicted
- VI. Losing your phone
- VII. The feeling of someone following you when it's dark out
- VIII. Liking a post on Instagram from 45 weeks ago
- IX. Waking up an hour after the alarm went off with a pang of horror
- X. Getting too close to the edge

ABSOLUTE STRANGERS

Whether on the street, in a cozy pub, on a plane, or waiting in line, here are some ideas of what to discuss with absolute strangers:

I. If they have any grandchildren
II. Where they get their coffee from
III. Rooftop bar locations
IV. Recommendations of where to go in the outskirts of the city
V. The current political climate
VI. Places to avoid
VII. Where to see the sunrise
VIII. How to navigate the metro
IX. Information regarding the current bank strike
X. Where to go out tonight

MOUNTAINS

Sometimes you have to endure a valley of mud to get to the top of your mountain.

You know you'll make it; that is never doubted. But tolerating the discomfort of the valley is what makes you hesitate and groan.

It's the climb that makes the destination so satisfying. The journey might have its happy moments, but usually, it's chaotic. It's scary. It's dirty. It's lonely. It's cruel and painful. It hurts.

We always make it to the top of the mountain, though.

And what does that say about us?

V. TRAVEL AS IMMORTALITY

The nitrogen in our DNA, the calcium in our teeth, the iron in our blood, the carbon in our apple pies were made in the interiors of collapsing stars. We are made of star stuff.

Carl Sagan

WRITING IT ALL DOWN

The passing sweet and sour moments are worth writing down.

You'll never forget the first time you see the Sagrada Familia or the Aqueduct of Segovia.

But will you remember the smell of the melted chocolate you dipped freshly baked churros in under the shadow of the Sagrada Familia?

Will you remember the name of the wine you drank with lunch as you gazed at the architectural grandeur of the aqueduct?

These little details are what charm your trips. Jotting them down on napkins or making notes in your phone will certainly put a smile on your face when you happen upon them months later.

If nothing else, travel notes will make an excellent first draft of your memoirs some day.

MUGSHOTS

When traveling, we have an inclination to take photographs of ourselves in front of noteworthy buildings, landmarks, and views. Going forward, these types of photos will be referred to as travel mugshots.

As seasoned travelers rack up their mugshots, they might wonder why they have these photographs taken in the first place. Why insert yourself into a picture of a wonderful structure? Is the photo you took of Big Ben really better with you in it? Does the Taj Mahal maintain its majesty when you pose in front of it? Why do people take these photographs of themselves so universally?

Here are some proposed explanations with superficiality in mind:
    I.   To hit the desired amount of likes on Instagram
    II.   To brag about being abroad to your less fortunate friends and enemies alike
    III. To show off how good you look

Here are other proposed explanations, without superficiality in mind:
    I.   For the grandkids
    II.   To later remind yourself of a delightful moment in a beautiful place
    III. To inspire your next trip

You decide.

TRAGEDY STRIKES

As you trot around the globe, you find yourself armed with an arsenal of travel mugshots. It would have been excessive to post all of them on social media during your trip, so you are left with a collection of could-be posts. Perhaps the photo of you in front of the Eiffel Tower beat the photo of you in front of Notre Dame. You sipping on tea in an outdoor cafe in Istanbul was more Instagrammable than you posing in front of the Hagia Sophia.

But, alas, tragedy strikes and you are given the opportunity to finally post those pictures. Notre Dame is burning down! You have that picture of yourself in front of it from two years ago on your solo trip to Paris. Terrorists have attacked the Hagia Sophia! You never thought you'd be able to post that picture.

You open Instagram, post the picture of yourself standing in front of the tragedy-stricken landmark.

#prayforparis #istanbulattacked

You feel content that you are able to raise awareness for the building's fate. You get a ton of likes because your followers want to show that they care about the tragedy, too. Everybody feels a little better.

Except the building itself and the people who are actually impacted by it. What about the casualties, the people who work there, or the people who witnessed it? These people are not comforted by the post of you looking glamorous in front of their cherished and hurt landmark. Vanity does not undo terrorism, reverse natural disasters, or repair trauma.

SING IN ME, MUSE

Greek Myth tells of nine muses.

Calliope, Epic Poetry
Clio, History
Erato, Lyric Poetry
Euterpe, Music
Melpomene, Tragedy
Polyhymnia, Sacred Poetry
Terpsichore, Dance & Chorus
Thalia, Comedy & Idyllic Poetry
Urania, Astronomy

Bring these ladies with you on your travels.

SCARS

Travel leaves scars on you.

On your body, maybe.

On your heart, definitely.

On your memory.

On your dreams.

On your judgment.

On your sense of reality.

On your sense of style.

On your interior decorating.

On your family and friends.

On your ambitions.

On your tolerance.

On your appreciation of life.

Never cover them up.

VI.
TRAVEL
AS
PHILOSOPHY

Know thyself. Nothing in excess.

Temple of Apollo, Delphi

!*#&

Learning a curse word in a foreign language is like God descending upon you from Heaven and whispering in your ear the meaning of life.

1492 SYNDROME

For each new place you visit, keep in mind that you are not the first person to go there. No matter how magical or novel it is, how enchanted you feel, or how wondrous your eyes gaze out on the new horizon, you are just a visitor staying for a while.

Arriving in a new land can make you feel like the Niña, Pinta, and Santa María that landed on Hispañola. The island was new and shiny to the conquistadors, but Taíno owned the ancient island.

Wherever you go, remember this about the locals. They go to school and they go to work. They buy their groceries and clean their houses. They raise their children and grow old. They are not on vacation. You are on their soil.

Keep that twinkle in your eye and don't be afraid to gasp in awe. But also keep the perspective that the locals and natives are your hosts and you are just passing by.

ODE TO ANTHONY BOURDAIN

In appreciation of one of the best travelers of our time, here are the revised Ten Commandments one must live by in order to avoid travel hell, as stated by the man himself.

I. "Your body is not a temple, it's an amusement park. Enjoy the ride."

II. "The journey is part of the experience, an expression of the seriousness of one's intent. One doesn't take the A Train to Mecca."

III. "You're never going to find a perfect city travel experience or the perfect meal without a constant willingness to experience a bad one."

IV. "Drink heavily with locals whenever possible."

V. "Nothing unexpected or wonderful is likely to happen if you have an itinerary in Paris filled with the Louvre and the Eiffel Tower."

VI. "Life, and travel, leaves marks on you. Most of the time, those marks, on your body or on your heart, are beautiful. Often, though, they hurt."

VII. "I know what I want. I want it all. I want to try everything once."

VIII. "It's an irritating reality that many places and events defy description."

IX. "In the end, you're just happy you were there, with your eyes open, and lived to see it."

X. "Travel is about the gorgeous feeling of teetering in the unknown."

grow up

grow tall

grow true

grow for you

grow deep down

grow wide

grow inside

grow apart

grow along side

grow and know

each trip

adds an inch

to your soul

ADVENTURE ANTITHESES

The hunger and the meal.

The athlete and the spectator.

The thirst and the quench.

The mortal and the immortal.

The sweatpants and the haute couture.

The injury and the rehab.

The subject and the artist.

KIR V. CŒUR

Unless your itinerary includes *Utter Embarrassment at the Café de Flore [10pm]*, then correct pronunciation should be on your packing list.

A waiter of Saint-Germain-des-Prés, specifically one who prides himself as an employee of Café de Flore, found it either annoying or amusing that I ordered a *cœur* one night in July. *How does one serve a heart?* he must have asked himself. Loyal to his duty, yet clearly not understanding what I wanted, and also clearly not speaking a word of English, he maintained his decorum and asked again what I would like to drink.

A heart, please, I said in French.

As I thumbed through the menu book to find the correct word, he racked his brain for what this American could possibly be asking for.

After what seemed like minutes I saw it. *Kir Royale*. There! Now he'll understand. I pointed to the menu.

He looked to where I pointed and shook his head, with only a hint of a smile on his face.

My education in French pronunciation was about to begin.

He said the word *cœur* the way I had tried to say *kir*, as he made the shape of a heart with his two pointer fingers.

A deep breath. And then.

He said *kir* with such passion that you'd think the word was his savior. He said it again, this time taking his right arm, bending it and forming a fist over his heart, looking out in the distance. *Kir!* He pronounced the word with such an irreplicable French accent, that not I nor half of France could mimic it.

This man, this saint, did not come to work that night to serve after-dinner beverages to the *flâneurs* of St. Germain. He came to defend his country.

THE ALLEGORY OF THE CAVE OF TRAVEL

Plato's Allegory of the Cave teaches of prisoners that experience just one reality. Chained inside a cave facing a wall, they can only see the shadows of whatever passes in front of a fire. They see the mere outline of what really exists. This is how they live.

One day, the prisoners escape their chains. They walk out of the cave and see the sun for the first time. They cannot comprehend the fire they now see. It is beyond their understanding of reality, a new realm of experience. They are blinded.

We are these prisoners until we travel. Trapped in a cave of just one reality, we cannot experience the higher realm until we break free. We don't even see what really exists. All we know are shadows, outlines, vague ideas.

Stepping out of the cave may blind you. It may expose you, force you into an uncomfortable place where you have no bearing of reality. You may lose control of your senses and what feels right.

But it is the only way to leave behind the one dimensional, dark world view of a prisoner. Get out of the cave, and look towards the light.

VII. TRAVEL AS HOME

We may value foreign elements not only because they are new but because they seem to accord more faithfully with our identity and commitments than anything our homeland can provide.

Alain de Botton

DREAMS

If you come home thinking it was all a dream, you might be right.

Not all dreams happen in your head.

SOUVENIRS

The Latin derivation of the word souvenir is *to occur in the mind*. Here are some of my favorite souvenirs from my trips abroad:

I. 17th century map of a small area in the Pyrenees where France and Spain border each other, purchased from the Marché aux Puces in Paris
II. A tiny bottle of organic Extra Virgin Olive Oil from the South of Spain
III. A blue pottery candlestick holder from a secondhand shop in Copenhagen
IV. Handwritten notes and tips from hosts, bartenders, absolute strangers, and friends
V. My favorite denim jacket, used and too large, from Malmö
VI. A tin of cloudberry candies from Holmenkollen
VII. Rosary beads for my grandmom, purchased at the Cathedral in Santiago de Compostela
VIII. A hand painted sangria pitcher from Salamanca for my mom
IX. Bottles of limoncello from the Amalfi Coast
X. Sleeves of Principe cookies
XI. Sardinas from abuela
XII. A postcard from every new city and country
XIII. A deeper taste for red wine
XIV. A marriage proposal on the streets of Stockholm
XV. A better appreciation for American toilets

In French

you don't say

I miss you.

You say

Tu me manques

which means

You are missing from me.

THE LONG DISTANCE RELATIONSHIP

If it's true love, it will be there waiting for you to come back.

And travel only knows true love.

ACKNOWLEDGMENTS

Thank you to:

Every pilot who has successfully flown me across an ocean | Every airport that sells 9 oz. glasses of wine | The absolute pleasure that traveling has given me | The lady on the train going from Barcelona to Salamanca who gave me napkins for the bathroom | The Dublin airport, which played *Celebrate* at the arrivals gate in March of 2014 | The city of Salamanca, inclusive of its University, residents, nightlife, and labyrinth road system | The entirety of Scandinavia. Its people, its lands, its beauty, its foods, and its gifts | My family, who has never stopped me from getting on a plane and has helped me get on many | The little zebra from Dad | La Familia Fernández por todo, por siempre. Yo podría escribir un libro sobre cada uno de vosotros, y todavía no sería bastante. | Anyone who has journeyed with me far and wide. Your patience has been extraordinary and your company has been everything. | The cathedrals of Spain. You know who you are. | La Quinta de Regaleira and the dreaminess of Sintra | Pedro | Loren | Gianpaolo | Tía y Gloria | The combination of mojitos + orthotics | The nice boy from Nice | The bartenders in Oslo that hand wrote weekend ideas for me on business cards and napkins | The stranger who proposed to me in Stockholm, regardless of whether it was a dare or not | My Guardian Angels for surely saving my life | Paulo Coelho | The way the sunlight hits Sacré-Cœur in the afternoon | The gentlemen on Las Ramblas in August of 2016 that helped me fix a cigarette machine at 4am | The doctor in Paris that was open on Bastille Day | Mallorca's red wine | Hautevillers's champagne houses | Scribe's pinot | Cañas | Free wifi in desperate places | The bachelor party in Brussels in 2017, where the groomsmen were accepting money from passersby to wax the groom's ass in public | The mind and heart of Anthony Bourdain

No thank you to:

The Swedish TSA for confiscating my tin of mussels from abuela | The high concentration of bicarbonate in many European bottled water companies that causes temporary, yet powerful, IBS | Anyone who suggested turning off the air conditioning or fans in the summer of 2015 | The bus line running from Antibes to Nice | The vagueness of where exactly Marie Antoinette's Estate is located on the grounds of Versailles, according to the visitor's map

ABOUT THE AUTHOR

Having spent every spare penny on travel since 2014, Katherine Scott's biggest regret is not traveling earlier. Her most important life lessons can be tied to a travel experience. She wants to spread travel awareness like some people spread Christmas cheer or political agendas.

Katherine lives by the beach and loves booking solo travel ventures while drinking red wine. She also loves her dog, mountains, and eating.

and when the child of morning,

rosy-fingered Dawn, appeared

they again set sail

The Iliad, Homer

This book is typeset in Cormorant Garamond.

hardship

travel

wild strength of will

joy

ᚷ
ᚱ
ᚨ
ᚹ

Made in the USA
Middletown, DE
20 April 2020